PRODUCTIVITY WITHOUT BURNOUT

BECOME YOUR MOST EFFICIENT SELF AND ACHIEVE STRESS-FREE ACCOMPLISHMENTS.

ALFRED CURTIN

All Rights Reserved. Alfred Curtin 2024

No part of this publication should be reproduced, stored in a retrieval system, or transmitted in any form or by any means—electronic, mechanical, photocopying, recording, scanning, or otherwise—except as permitted without the prior written permission of the author.

TABLE OF CONTENT

INTRODUCTION 5
    UNDERSTANDING TRUE PRODUCTIVITY 7
    THE ILLUSION OF PRODUCTIVITY 9

Chapter 1 14

STRATEGIES FOR EFFECTIVE TASK MANAGEMENT 14
    PRIORITIZE LESS 14
    WORK AT YOUR NATURAL PACE 16
    PRIORITIZE QUALITY OVER QUANTITY 17

Chapter 2 20

THE IMPORTANCE OF BREAKS AND REST 20
    BIOLOGICAL BENEFITS 20
    PSYCHOLOGICAL BENEFITS: 21
    INCORPORATING REST FOR LONG-TERM EFFICIENCY 22

Chapter 3 24

MINDFULNESS AND FOCUS 24
    CULTIVATING PRESENT MOMENT AWARENESS FOR GREATER FOCUS 26
    CREATING A SUSTAINABLE WORK ENVIRONMENT 28
    DESIGNING YOUR WORKSPACE FOR PRODUCTIVITY AND WELL-BEING 30

Chapter 4 33

STRATEGIES FOR DEALING WITH OVERWHELM AND BURNOUT 33

Conclusion 36

INTRODUCTION

Cohen was a young man living in a lively metropolis. Cohen was ambitious and hardworking, with aspirations of great success in his career. However, he was frequently overwhelmed by the responsibilities of his profession and the need to perform consistently at a high level.

Cohen stumbled across this book one day and was intrigued. He began to read it in the hopes of finding some advice on how to better manage his workload.

As he read through the book, Cohen discovered a variety of practical ways to increase productivity without jeopardizing his well-being. He learned the value of setting achievable goals, prioritizing chores, and taking regular breaks to recharge. He also learned the significance of mindfulness and self-care in achieving a healthy work-life balance.

Inspired by what he had read, Cohen began to apply these concepts in his daily life. He began defining specific, attainable goals for himself and dividing his duties into smaller, more doable chunks.

He also made a concerted effort to take many breaks during the day, giving himself time to relax and rejuvenate.

To his amazement, Cohen discovered that he could accomplish more in less time and under less stress. He had grown more productive by putting the book's teachings into practice without overloading himself. He was able to accomplish his goals while simultaneously caring for his mental and physical health.

As time passed, Cohen's coworkers noticed a shift in him. He was more focused, efficient, and optimistic about his work. His productivity had increased, but more importantly, he felt happier.

Cohen recognized that true productivity is not about working harder or longer hours, but about working better and more sustainably. He had discovered a road to long-term productivity and became his most efficient self by putting the teachings of this book into practice. As he continued on his quest, he was confident that he would meet his objectives without burning out.

UNDERSTANDING TRUE PRODUCTIVITY

The concept of productivity frequently conjures up images of frenetic schedules, never-ending to-do lists, and a relentless quest for efficiency. True productivity, however, extends beyond merely completing more tasks in less time. It takes a comprehensive approach to work and life, emphasizing performance, fulfillment, and well-being.

True productivity is fundamentally about connecting our actions with our values and priorities. It's about understanding that productivity is more than just performing more activities; it's about doing the appropriate jobs—the ones that get us closer to our goals and fulfill us on a deeper level. This requires the ability to distinguish between busy work and meaningful work, as well as a realization that not all activities are created equal.

While busy work can keep us engaged, it frequently diverts our attention away from what is truly important. It can create a sensation of busyness without actual progress, leaving us fatigued and unfulfilled. On the other hand, meaningful labor is consistent with our beliefs and adds to our long-term objectives. It provides a sense of purpose and accomplishment, fueling rather than exhausting us.

Another important part of actual productivity is understanding how our priorities and values influence how we spend our time. When our activities are consistent with our values, we are more likely to feel inspired and engaged at work. Dissatisfaction and fatigue can result from a disconnect between our behaviors and values.

Furthermore, our thinking plays an important part in increasing productivity. A growth mindset, defined as the concept that our talents can be developed through effort and dedication, can help us overcome obstacles and remain resilient in the face of failures.

On the other side, a fixed mindset, defined by the notion that our talents are intrinsic and immutable, can lead to feelings of helplessness and stagnation.

In essence, great productivity does not need working harder or longer hours.

It's about working smarter—prioritizing tasks that correspond with our beliefs, creating a development mindset, and striking a balance that allows us to achieve our goals while without jeopardizing our well-being.

Understanding and embracing true productivity allows us to become our most efficient selves and achieve stress-free goals.

THE ILLUSION OF PRODUCTIVITY

There is a pervasive illusion of productivity that frequently steers us away from actual effectiveness and efficiency. This illusion, known as pseudo-productivity, entails participating in activities that appear to be productive but do not contribute meaningfully to our goals or well-being

The growth in pseudo-productivity can be ascribed to a variety of factors, including societal pressures to be always active, the celebration of multitasking, and the belief that more labor equals more achievement. As a result, many people find themselves imprisoned in a never-ending cycle of busyness, chasing tasks and deadlines without pausing to assess if these activities are genuinely important or useful.

One of the distinguishing features of pseudo-productivity is the tendency to prioritize numbers over quality.

This can appear in a variety of ways, including focusing on completing a large number of activities fast rather than taking the time to complete them effectively, or engaging in busy work to fill our calendars without making progress toward our goals.

Another typical feature of pseudo-productivity is the emphasis on surface-level measurements of success, such as the number of hours worked or the length of our to-do lists, rather than the impact or significance of our efforts. This can provide a sense of accomplishment in the short term, but it usually leads to burnout and discontent in the long run.

The fall of pseudo-productivity is evident when we discover that, despite our hectic schedules and long hours, we are not making significant progress toward our goals. We may feel overwhelmed, frustrated, and unfulfilled, wondering why our efforts appear to generate few results.

To overcome the illusion of productivity, we must learn to emphasize quality over quantity, focusing on tasks that are consistent with our values and aspirations. This may necessitate saying no to activities or commitments that do not serve our purpose, to focus our time and energy on important activities.

Furthermore, we must learn to accept a slower, more thoughtful approach to work, understanding that true productivity is measured not by how much we can do in a day, but by how efficiently we can achieve our goals over time. We may build a more sustainable and fulfilling work environment by reevaluating our approach to productivity and letting go of the illusion of busyness.

Embracing a Slower, More Sustainable Approach

The concept of slowing down may appear paradoxical to productivity. However, adopting a calmer, more sustainable attitude to work and life is critical for preventing burnout and long-term success.

There is an ongoing pressure to do more, accomplish more, and be more productive. However, the unrelenting pursuit of productivity can sometimes result in burnout, stress, and a sense of being continually overburdened. Embracing a slower, more sustainable approach to work and life should not imply laziness or inefficiency. Instead, it's about being deliberate with our time and energy, prioritizing what's genuinely important, and striking a balance that allows us to be both productive and healthy.

One of the primary advantages of taking a slower approach is the option to prioritize quality over quantity. When we slow down and take the time to do things correctly, we can create higher-quality work that is more important and effective. This can lead to greater happiness and a sense of achievement, even if we are unable to accomplish as much in the same amount of time.

At its foundation, adopting a slower pace is being deliberate about how we spend our time and energy.

It entails understanding that productivity is more than simply getting things done quickly; it is also about doing them properly and in a way that protects our well-being.

One important part of adopting a slower pace is learning to prioritize our responsibilities and obligations. Instead of attempting to tackle everything at once, we can concentrate on a few important objectives that are consistent with our values and aims. This enables us to allocate our time and energy more effectively, resulting in increased total productivity.

Another crucial part of adopting a slower approach is learning to pace oneself.

This entails realizing that our energy levels change throughout the day and that it is acceptable to take pauses as needed. By listening to our body and allowing ourselves to rest, we may avoid burnout and maintain a consistent level of productivity.

Taking a slower approach also entails being aware of our work habits and routines.

This entails paying attention to how we operate best and fostering an environment that encourages productivity. This could include creating boundaries around our work hours, reducing distractions, and taking regular pauses to refuel.

Finally, adopting a slower, more sustainable approach to work and life entails striking a balance that allows us to achieve our objectives without jeopardizing our well-being. We may avoid burnout and achieve stress-free accomplishments by being deliberate about how we use our time and energy, pacing ourselves, and creating a work atmosphere that encourages productivity.

Chapter 1

STRATEGIES FOR EFFECTIVE TASK MANAGEMENT

PRIORITIZE LESS

In our desire for productivity, we frequently fall into the trap of attempting to do too much. We cram our schedules with countless duties and responsibilities, convinced that the more we accomplish, the more successful we will become. However, this method can result in exhaustion, burnout, and a sensation of constant busyness.

Prioritizing less does not imply being lazy or ignoring our responsibilities. Instead, it entails being careful about the tasks and obligations we accept, focusing solely on those that are consistent with our aims and beliefs. Prioritizing less allows us to attain more meaningful results while also reducing stress.

One of the primary advantages of prioritizing less is the opportunity to focus on what is genuinely important. With fewer chores on our plate, we can spend more time and focus on each one, ensuring that we complete them thoroughly and effectively. This can result in higher-quality work and a stronger sense of success, even if we can't produce as much overall.

Another benefit to focusing less is the capacity to avoid fatigue. When we consistently overload ourselves with responsibilities and commitments, we risk depleting our mental and physical resources. Prioritizing less allows us to have adequate time and energy to rest and recharge, resulting in increased overall productivity and well-being.

Prioritizing less allows us to be more flexible and adaptable at work.

When we are not burdened with a huge list of duties, we can respond more effectively to unanticipated difficulties and opportunities as they emerge. This can lead to a higher sense of control over our job and a more positive attitude towards new situations.

Finally, prioritizing less is a highly successful work management method. We can achieve more meaningful results, prevent burnout, and feel more satisfied with our jobs and lives if we focus only on what genuinely counts.

WORK AT YOUR NATURAL PACE

In the pursuit of productivity, there is often a temptation to work quicker and harder, believing that this would lead to greater success. However, this technique can sometimes result in burnout and decreased efficiency. Working at your natural speed, on the other hand, entails understanding your rhythms and energy levels and adjusting your workload accordingly. This method can result in increased productivity, higher-quality work, and a more sustainable work-life balance.

One of the primary advantages of working at your natural pace is the ability to keep a steady level of energy and focus throughout the day. Paying attention to your body's natural rhythms allows you to schedule your most difficult work when you are most alert and concentrated while saving less demanding jobs for times when your energy levels are low. This can help you avoid the mid-afternoon slump and be more productive throughout the day.

Another benefit of working at your natural pace is the ability to prevent burnout. When you force yourself to work at an unsustainable rate, you risk depleting yourself both mentally and physically. Working at a comfortable and sustainable pace will help you prevent burnout and maintain a healthy work-life balance.

Working at your natural pace allows you to be more present and involved with your task. When you are continually rushing, it may be difficult to concentrate fully on the subject at hand, resulting in diminished productivity and lower-quality work. Working at your natural pace allows you to be more present and attentive, resulting in higher-quality work and greater satisfaction with your results.

Working at your natural pace is an important method for good task management. Understanding your rhythms and energy levels allows you to schedule your work in a way that improves productivity and efficiency while also promoting a good work–life balance.

PRIORITIZE QUALITY OVER QUANTITY

There is a strong emphasis on quantity—the more chores we can perform, the more successful we are thought to be. However, this concentration on quantity can also compromise quality.

Prioritizing quality above quantity entails altering our perspective to focus on the impact and worth of our labor, rather than the sheer number of activities we can complete.

One of the primary advantages of emphasizing quality over number is the potential to create work that is significant and influential. When we focus on doing a few things well, rather than trying to do everything, we can spend more time and attention on each activity, resulting in higher-quality outcomes. When we see the tangible consequences of our work, we feel more satisfied and accomplished.

Another benefit of favoring quality over quantity is the potential to save time and energy in the long run. When we speed through activities to do as many as possible, we may neglect critical details or make mistakes that take more time and effort to remedy. Taking the time to do things correctly the first time can help us avoid costly mistakes and save time in the long term.

Prioritizing quality over number allows us to focus on what is truly important. When we are not weighed down by a huge list of duties, we can focus on the most important and effective work, ensuring that our efforts are in line with our aims and values.

This can lead to a higher sense of purpose and fulfillment in our work, as we can see how our efforts affect our overall performance.

Finally, choosing quality over number is an important method for good work management. By focusing on delivering high-quality, meaningful, and effective work, we can increase our success and satisfaction while avoiding burnout and overwhelm.

Chapter 2

THE IMPORTANCE OF BREAKS AND REST

The importance of taking breaks and obtaining appropriate rest is sometimes ignored. However, breaks and rest are necessary to preserve productivity, creativity, and overall well-being. In this chapter, we will look at the biological and psychological benefits of taking pauses and rest, as well as techniques for implementing them into our daily lives to achieve stress-free results.

BIOLOGICAL BENEFITS

Energy Restoration: Taking breaks helps our bodies to relax and recover, which replenishes our energy levels. This can reduce weariness and increase overall productivity.

Stress Reduction: Taking breaks and getting enough rest can help our bodies produce less cortisol, the stress hormone. This can alleviate emotions of worry and stress.

Improved Concentration: Rest is vital for our bodies' ability to repair and rebuild cells. A lack of rest can weaken the immune system, increasing the risk of sickness.

PSYCHOLOGICAL BENEFITS:

Enhanced Creativity: Breaks can boost creativity by allowing our minds to wander and explore new ideas. This can result in new perspectives and imaginative solutions to challenges.

Mood Improvement: Taking breaks allows us to rest and unwind, which improves our mood. This can result in a higher level of well-being and happiness.

Memory Consolidation: Rest is essential for memory consolidation, the process by which memories are reinforced and stored. Taking breaks between study or work periods will help you retain more knowledge.

Increased Productivity: Contrary to popular opinion, taking breaks can boost productivity. Allowing our brains and bodies to rest allows us to return to work feeling refreshed and ready to take on new challenges.

Including breaks and respite in our every day routines is critical for maintaining productivity, creativity, and general well-being. Recognizing the biological and psychological benefits of breaks and relaxation allows us to prioritize these important practices and achieve stress-free results.

INCORPORATING REST FOR LONG-TERM EFFICIENCY

Rest is sometimes viewed as a luxury rather than a necessity. However, incorporating rest into our every day routines is critical for long-term efficiency and productivity. In this chapter, we will look at the necessity of rest for long-term efficiency and examine how to incorporate it into our everyday routines.

Preventing Burnout: Rest is critical for avoiding burnout, a state of emotional, bodily, and mental weariness produced by chronic stress. Regular rest can help us avoid burnout and maintain a high level of efficiency over time.

Improving Cognitive Function: Rest is essential for cognitive function, which includes memory, focus, and problem-solving ability.

Taking breaks and getting enough sleep can help us think clearly and make better judgments, resulting in greater efficiency at work.

Rest can boost creativity by allowing our minds to wander and form new connections. Taking breaks and allowing ourselves to relax can result in new thoughts and innovative solutions to issues, increasing our overall efficiency.

Boosting Physical Health: Rest is necessary for immunological function, metabolism, and overall well-being. Getting enough rest can help us avoid disease and accomplish our everyday tasks more efficiently.

Strategies to Incorporate Rest:

Schedule Regular Breaks: Include brief breaks throughout your workday to rest and refuel. Use this opportunity to stretch, take a walk, or do something soothing.

Prioritize Sleep: Get adequate sleep every night so your body and mind can rest and rejuvenate. Aim for 7-9 hours of quality sleep per night.

Incorporating mindfulness activities into your everyday routine, such as meditation or deep breathing exercises, can help you relax and reduce stress.

Set boundaries: Learn to say no to projects or commitments that will disrupt your sleep and well-being. Prioritize your health and well-being before all else.

Rest is vital for long-term efficiency and production. Recognizing the importance of rest and applying techniques to include it in our routines allows us to achieve stress-free success while maintaining a high level of efficiency over time.

Chapter 3

MINDFULNESS AND FOCUS

Maintaining focus and productivity in today's society is difficult due to distractions. However, mindfulness offers a significant answer to this difficulty. Mindfulness is the practice of remaining fully present and aware of one's thoughts, feelings, and environment without judgment.

By adding mindfulness into our daily lives, we may improve our focus, and productivity, and perform tasks without stress.

Mindfulness improves attention by training our thoughts to remain present and avoid distractions. Mindfulness helps us become more aware of our thoughts and emotions, allowing us to respond to them in a calm and regulated manner. This increased awareness allows us to concentrate on the work at hand and avoid being distracted by unnecessary thoughts or stimuli.

Furthermore, mindfulness has been demonstrated to improve cognitive functions such as remembering, problem-solving, and decision-making.

By practicing mindfulness, we can increase our cognitive capacities, making it easier to stay focused and productive at work and in our daily lives.

One of the primary advantages of mindfulness is its capacity to alleviate tension and anxiety. When we're worried, our minds wander, making it harder to focus. Mindfulness can help us relax our brains and minimize stress, allowing us to maintain attention and productivity.

There are a variety of ways to incorporate mindfulness into our daily lives. Simple activities like mindful breathing, which involves focusing on our breath and observing our thoughts without judgment, can help us grow awareness. In addition, practices like yoga and meditation can help us build attention and focus.

Overall, mindfulness is an effective strategy for boosting focus, increasing productivity, and accomplishing tasks without stress.

By adopting mindfulness into our daily routines, we may create a more focused and productive attitude, resulting in better success and fulfillment in our careers and lives.

CULTIVATING PRESENT MOMENT AWARENESS FOR GREATER FOCUS

In our fast-paced, technology-driven society, it's easy to get caught up in the continual flood of information and diversions. However, practicing present-moment awareness might help us focus and be more productive. Present moment awareness, also known as mindfulness, entails being completely present and engaged in the present moment, free of judgment or distraction. By strengthening this awareness, we can improve our capacity to focus, make better decisions, and execute tasks without stress.

One of the most important components of developing present-moment awareness is learning to quiet the mind and focus on the current moment.

This can be accomplished through practices such as meditation, in which we focus our attention on our breath or a mantra, helping us to become more aware of our thoughts and feelings while avoiding getting caught up in them. By practicing meditation daily, we may train our minds to remain focused and present in the face of distractions.

Another crucial part of developing present-moment awareness is learning to let go of the past and future.

We often get caught up in ruminating about the past or worrying about the future, which can take our attention away from the current moment. By practicing mindfulness, we can learn to let go of these ideas and focus our attention on the here and now, boosting our capacity to stay focused and productive.

Cultivating present-moment awareness can also help us become more aware of our habits and patterns of behavior. By being attentive to our behaviors and reactions, we can recognize any unhelpful habits that may be impeding our productivity and make changes as needed.

For example, we may recognize that when presented with difficult work, we tend to procrastinate; by being aware of this tendency, we may take steps to resist it and stay focused on the current task.

Overall, fostering present-moment awareness is an effective way to improve focus, productivity, and overall well-being. By learning to calm the mind, let go of the past and future, and become more conscious of our patterns, we may improve our capacity to stay focused and achieve our goals more easily and efficiently.

CREATING A SUSTAINABLE WORK ENVIRONMENT

A sustainable work environment prioritizes productivity, well-being, and long-term success. It is an environment in which employees feel valued, engaged, and motivated to perform their best. In this section, we'll look at how to build a sustainable work environment that promotes productivity and well-being for everyone.

1. Create a culture of respect and collaboration:

Encourage open communication, respect for other viewpoints, and a collaborative approach to work. This promotes a healthy and supportive work atmosphere in which people feel valued and inspired to contribute.

2. Improve Work-Life Balance:

Encourage employees to put their well-being first by fostering work-life balance. This can include providing flexible work arrangements, encouraging time off, and discouraging excessive labor.

3. Provide Opportunities for Growth and Development:

Invest in staff development by providing training, mentorship programs, and growth opportunities.

This makes employees feel valued and motivated to advance in the organization.

4. Establish a Healthy Physical Environment:

Make sure the workspace is pleasant, well-lit, and devoid of risks. Consider air quality, temperature, and noise levels while designing a healthy and effective work environment.

5. Support Employee Well-Being:

Provide resources and support for employee well-being, including mental health services, wellness initiatives, and ergonomic workspaces. This makes employees feel more supported and valued, leading to higher job satisfaction and productivity.

6. Encourage sustainable practices:

Encourage sustainable practices within the organization, such as recycling, waste reduction, and the use of energy-efficient equipment. This contributes to the development of a sustainable culture while also demonstrating a commitment to environmental responsibility.

7. Recognize and reward success.

Recognize and celebrate staff successes to create a positive and stimulating work environment. This may involve formal recognition programs, bonuses, or other incentives.

8. Embrace Diversity and Inclusion

Create a workplace that is inclusive and welcoming to employees from all backgrounds. This can encourage creativity, innovation, and teamwork, resulting in a more productive and successful organization.

DESIGNING YOUR WORKSPACE FOR PRODUCTIVITY AND WELL-BEING

The workplace has a significant impact on our productivity, creativity, and overall well-being. A well-designed workspace may motivate us, reduce stress, and improve our capacity to concentrate and perform at our peak. In this section, we'll look at how to design a workspace that encourages productivity and well-being, regardless of the type of job you do.

1. Select a Dedicated Workspace.

Set aside a separate space from your home or business for work. This helps to create a separation between your professional and personal lives, allowing you to focus when you're at work and relax when you're not.

2. Consider ergonomics:

Ensure that your workspace is pleasant and promotes healthy posture.

This includes using a chair that provides adequate back support, a desk that is the appropriate height, and proper lighting to reduce eye strain.

3. Personalize Your Space:

Personalize your office by adding photos, artwork, or plants. These can contribute to a sense of comfort and familiarity in your workstation, making it feel more inviting and inspirational.

4. Minimize distractions:

Identify and reduce potential distractions in your workstation, such as noise and clutter. This could include utilizing noise-canceling headphones, organizing your workspace, or establishing boundaries with others in your home or business.

5. Incorporate Nature.

Bring nature into your workspace by incorporating plants or natural materials. According to research, spending time in nature can improve mood, reduce stress, and boost creativity.

6. Design a functional layout:

Arrange your workspace to be functional and productive. This could involve keeping commonly used objects easily accessible, organizing your workplace to reduce clutter, and designating separate zones for different tasks.

7. Prioritize comfort.

Make your workstation more comfortable by investing in a supportive chair, using a desk that is the appropriate height for you, and including items like a footrest or ergonomic keyboard and mouse.

8. Apply Color Psychology:

Choose colors for your workspace that have been shown to increase productivity and well-being. For example, blue is associated with tranquility and concentration, whereas green is associated with creativity and balance.

Designing your workstation with these concepts in mind allows you to create a space that not only increases productivity but also promotes general well-being.

A well-designed office can help you achieve your goals while also promoting a good work-life balance.

Chapter 4

STRATEGIES FOR DEALING WITH OVERWHELM AND BURNOUT

Overwhelm and burnout are typical in today's fast-paced environment, but they are not unavoidable. By employing effective tactics, you may manage overwhelm and minimize burnout, allowing you to achieve your goals more easily while maintaining a good work-life balance.

Feeling overwhelmed is a regular occurrence in today's fast-paced society. The incessant pressures of work, family, and other duties can leave us feeling pressured, nervous, and unprepared to manage. However, we can overcome overwhelm and reclaim control and balance in our lives.

In this section, we'll look at ways for dealing with overwhelm and burnout.

1. Recognize Signs: Recognizing the symptoms of overwhelm and burnout is the first step in overcoming them. These symptoms may include feeling continually agitated, tired, angry, or unable to concentrate. Pay attention to these indications and take action to correct them.

2. Practice Self-Compassion: Be nice to yourself and accept that it's normal to feel overwhelmed at times. Avoid self-criticism and negative self-talk, and instead, practice self-compassion by treating yourself with the same care and understanding as you would a friend.

3. Set Boundaries: - Learn to say no to unnecessary chores or commitments when feeling overwhelmed. Prioritize your well-being and schedule time for activities that will recharge you.

4. Practice mindfulness to handle stress and overwhelm by focusing on the present moment. Deep breathing, meditation, or yoga are all examples of mindfulness exercises that can help you relax and relieve stress.

5. Break down tasks into smaller steps: large jobs can be stressful, but breaking them down into smaller, more manageable steps can help them appear more doable. Focus on finishing one step at a time rather than attempting to complete the full activity at once.

6. Seek Support: If you are feeling overwhelmed or burned out, do not hesitate to seek help from friends, family, or a mental health professional. Talking with others can help you gain perspective and identify solutions.

7. Take Breaks and Rest: - Schedule regular breaks and get enough rest. Taking pauses can help revitalize your mind and body, resulting in increased productivity in the long run.

8. Evaluate and Adjust: - Regularly assess your workload and commitments to ensure they are manageable. Adjust your schedule or priorities as needed to lessen overwhelm and avoid burnout.

Implementing these tactics will help you deal with overwhelm and burnout, allowing you to achieve your goals more easily and maintain a healthy work-life balance. Remember to prioritize your well-being and seek help if needed.

Conclusion

The goal of productivity frequently has a negative impact on our health. We push ourselves to do more, work harder, and reach new heights, frequently overlooking the need for balance and sustainability. True productivity, on the other hand, is defined by working smarter and more sustainably, not harder or longer hours.

we looked at ways to increase productivity without jeopardizing our health, happiness, or overall well-being. We've discovered that sustainable productivity is more than just getting things done; it's about doing them in a way that allows us to preserve a feeling of balance and fulfillment in our lives.

Prioritizing self-care is an important element of long-term productivity. Taking care of oneself physically, psychologically, and emotionally is critical for maintaining high productivity and preventing burnout. We've also learnt the value of setting realistic objectives, practicing mindfulness, being flexible, seeking help, and enjoying our accomplishments along the road.

By incorporating these ideas into our daily lives, we can attain our goals more easily and efficiently, while also maintaining a healthy work-life balance. We can achieve our full potential without succumbing to burnout.

As we complete this book, remember that productivity is a marathon, not a sprint. It's about pacing ourselves, listening to our bodies and brains, and being gentle with ourselves along the journey. By adopting sustainable productivity techniques, we can live more happy lives, achieve our goals, and ultimately attain the balance we all want.

www.ingramcontent.com/pod-product-compliance
Lightning Source LLC
Chambersburg PA
CBHW070956220526
45471CB00007B/3055